I0814239

Dog Projects

BY MARIE PEARSON

Kids Core
An Imprint of Abdo Publishing
abdobooks.com

abdobooks.com

Printed in the United States of America, North Mankato, Minnesota.
102025
012026

Cover Photo: Utekhina Anna/Shutterstock Images
Interior Photos: Elena Yakimova/Shutterstock Images, 4–5; Shutterstock Images, 7, 10, 12–13, 26 (top left, bottom right), 26 (top right), 26 (bottom left), 29 (bottom); kali9/E+/Getty Images, 8; Rita Kochmarjova/Shutterstock Images, 14; Roman Zaiets/Shutterstock Images, 17; Maria Moroz/Shutterstock Images, 18; Eva Blanco/Shutterstock Images, 20–21; Ermolaev Alexander/Shutterstock Images, 23; Manu Vega/Moment/Getty Images, 24; Thirawatana Phaisalratana/Shutterstock Images, 28 (top); Evgeny Atamanenko/Shutterstock Images, 28 (bottom); Anna Hoychuk/Shutterstock Images, 29 (top)

Editors: Rebecca Higgins and Trudy Becker
Series Designer: Marley Richmond

Library of Congress Control Number: 2025939247

Publisher's Cataloging-in-Publication Data

Names: Pearson, Marie, author.
Title: Dog projects / by Marie Pearson
Description: Minneapolis, Minnesota: Abdo Publishing, 2026 | Series: Citizen science projects | Includes online resources and index.
Identifiers: ISBN 9781098298562 (lib. bdg.) | ISBN 9798384932369 (ebook)
Subjects: LCSH: Science projects--Juvenile literature. | Field experiments--Juvenile literature. | Dogs--Juvenile literature. | Zoology--Experiments--Juvenile literature. | Zoology--Juvenile literature. | Ecology--Experiments--Juvenile literature. | Ecological science--Juvenile literature.
Classification: DDC 507.8--dc23

CONTENTS

In 2025, more than 65 million households in the United States had at least one dog.

Studying How Dogs Age

Lily and her grandpa sat down in the library's meeting room. Other kids and adults filled the room. Lily and her grandpa had just finished making a fleece rope toy for their dog, Pronto. Now an instructor named Henry stood at the front of the room.

He said every dog owner there could help dogs. They could do it by joining the Dog Aging Project (DAP).

Henry explained that the DAP is a dog health study. Dog owners across the United States give information about their dogs to scientists. They answer questions about their dogs' energy levels, playing **habits**, diet, and more. Scientists use this **data** to better understand dog health and aging. They use it to help study human aging too.

Lily asked her grandpa, "Can we join the project with Pronto?"

He smiled. "Of course."

Henry handed Lily and her grandpa an information packet. The packet listed a website.

Scientists around the world can use data from the Dog Aging Project.

Dogs of all types are welcome in DAP studies. Owners just need to have a good idea of their dog's current age to join.

They could join the DAP on the site. Lily couldn't wait to get home and answer the questions about Pronto with her grandpa. She had always loved her dog. Now she had a chance to help many dogs!

Citizen Science with Dogs

The DAP is one of many citizen science projects. Anyone can be a citizen scientist by collecting data for researchers. Kids can often do citizen science projects, though they might need to work with a trusted adult.

Researchers are not always able to collect all the data they need. Citizen scientists can help. They can gather even more information.

Aging Speed

Dogs age much faster than humans. Because of this, it is easier to study aging in dogs than it is in humans. Scientists can get answers to their questions about aging sooner. That way, they can use the information to help humans too.

Some dog projects may study the same dogs for months or years. Others collect data just once.

That information helps researchers answer questions about the world. Several projects are focused on dogs. Citizen scientists can collect data about dogs that helps both dogs and people.

Kate Creevy, cofounder of the DAP, said:

> This is a really important example of community science. The people collecting the scientific data for the Dog Aging Project are . . . everyday folks. . . . Science is happening all the time all around us.

Source: "Dog Aging Project Aims to Prolong Canine Lifespans." *YouTube*, uploaded by CBS TEXAS, 6 Feb. 2025, youtube.com. Accessed 22 Mar. 2025.

Comparing Texts

Think about the quote. Does it support the information in this chapter? Or does it give a different perspective? Explain how in a few sentences.

The average lifespan of a dog is between 10 and 13 years.

Dog Health Projects

The DAP is one of many citizen science projects that studies **canine** health. Dogs face many of the same health challenges as people. The findings from these studies could help both dogs and people live longer and healthier lives.

Living in clean and safe areas can help dogs live longer lives.

Genetics, lifestyle, and **environment** all play a big role in a dog's health and length of life. For example, certain genetics make dogs more likely to get cancer or other diseases. A dog's size and activity level can affect its health. So can some chemicals in the home.

Dog owners send information about these things to the DAP. They might give their dog's body measurements. They might collect **DNA** samples. To do that, an owner rubs a swab in the dog's mouth. Then they mail it to the DAP. Owners may send videos of their dogs. When owners bring their dog to the vet, they can get a blood sample to send in. Scientists use this data to learn how to help dogs live longer and healthier lives.

Darwin's Ark

Darwin's Ark is another citizen science project studying dog health. Dog owners answer questions about their pet's health, environment, and more. Owners also send in DNA. Scientists study this information. They have already made discoveries. For example, they found that

Healthy Dogs Help Research

Many dog owners walk their pets. This helps dogs stay healthy and happy. Owners can help nature while doing this. They can bring along a phone with the iNaturalist app. They can take photos of wildlife and plants. Then they can upload the photos to the app. This helps researchers track the area's health and the species that live there.

Most dogs need one or two walks a day.

certain genes make a dog more likely to get some cancers. That information helps scientists improve medical care. Care can get better for both dogs and people.

Research using Darwin's Ark data has shown that dogs and humans get bone cancer from the same changes to genes.

The program also studies how a dog's environment affects cancer risk. In one study, Darwin's Ark sent some owners a special tag. It was made of a material called silicone.

Silicone traps chemicals that are in the air. Later, owners mailed back the tags.

Scientists began to study the chemicals in the tags. They wanted to learn which chemicals were in different houses. This information can help researchers find out if certain chemicals are a risk to dogs and humans.

Explore Online

Visit the website below. Does it give any new information about dog health research that wasn't in Chapter Two?

Dog Aging Project: Our Mission

abdocorelibrary.com/dog-projects

Some dogs may wait by the door when they are left home alone.

CHAPTER 3

Dog Behavior Projects

Darwin's Ark doesn't only study dog health. It also studies dog **behavior**. Some dogs do not behave well. For example, dogs may panic when left home alone. Or they may bite people or other dogs. These issues can be hard for dogs and owners.

They may make dogs hard to live with. So, some people want to make these issues less common.

Other dog behaviors make life with dogs easier. Many people want dogs that are friendly. For example, they may want their dogs to get along with pet cats. People hope to make positive traits such as these more common in dogs.

Scientists have found many factors that affect dog behavior. Genetics can make a difference. So can the way a dog was raised. Getting enough exercise can affect behavior too. People can help with this research. In Darwin's Ark, owners answer questions about their dogs. They can even send in DNA. Then researchers learn more about how dogs think and act.

Some dogs get along well with other animals.

Canine Brains and C-BARQ

Harvard University in Massachusetts runs the Canine Brains Project. The project's goal is to understand how dog brains work. Dog owners answer questions online.

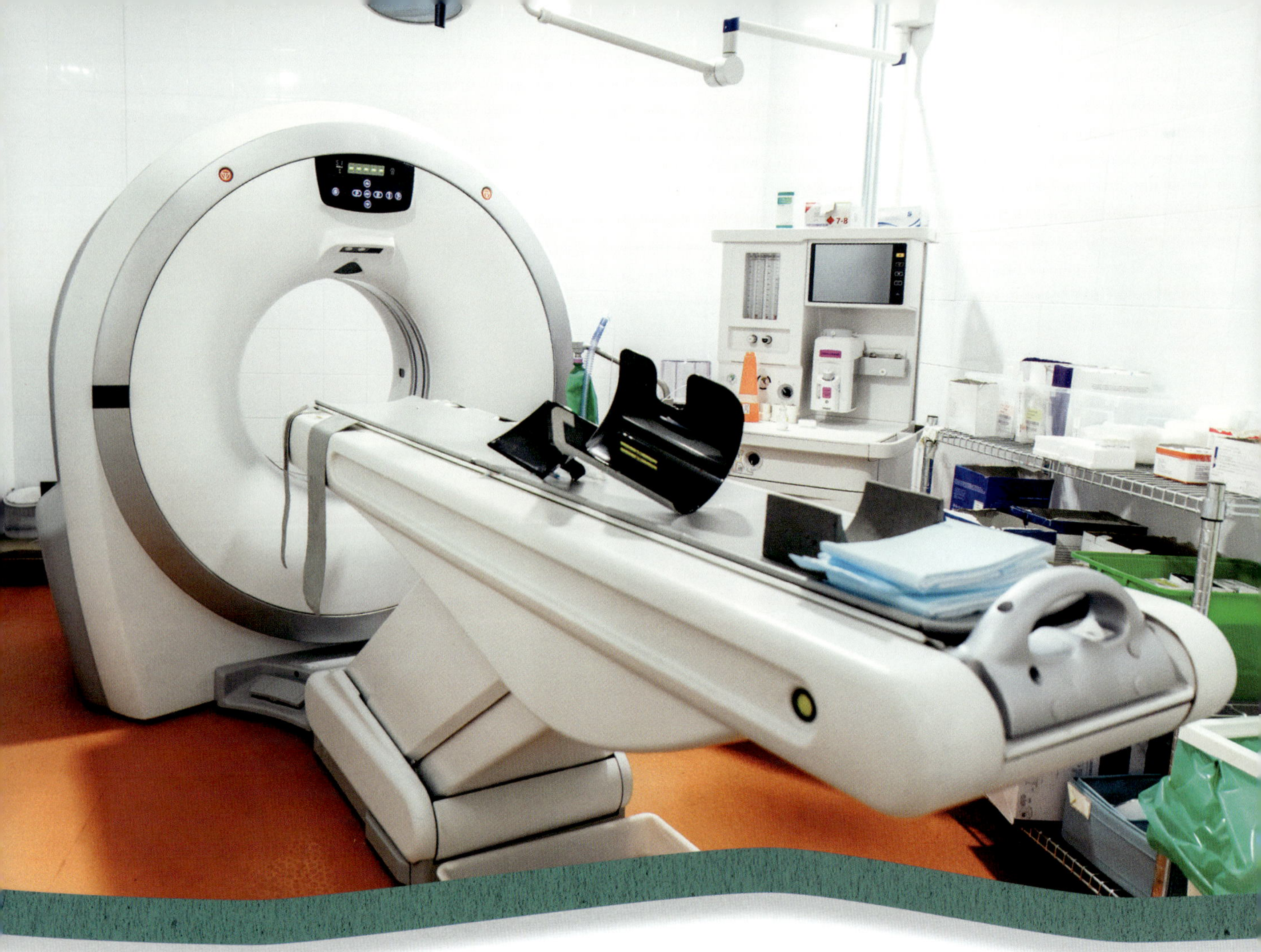

MRI machines take scans of dogs' brains. Then researchers and veterinarians can study the scans.

They can also bring their dogs to the university. The dogs get brain scans there.

Researchers hope to learn how dogs' brains are different depending on the jobs they were bred to do. Those jobs can include herding or retrieving. Scientists also want to know how living with children affects dogs.

Another tool used for dog behavior research is the Canine Behavioral Assessment and Research Questionnaire (C-BARQ). Owners answer questions about their dog's behavior. The owners get an immediate score. They can see where their dogs rank on factors such as **aggression**, fear, and other behaviors.

A Dog's Mind

In 2024, Netflix released a documentary called *Inside the Mind of a Dog*. It features the Canine Brains Project and other dog research projects. The show includes tips. It helps owners form good relationships with their dogs.

Answering Questions about Dogs

Citizen scientists may need to share important pieces of information about their dogs for research projects.

The C-BARQ stores all the data. Researchers such as those at the DAP can use it to learn how common certain behavioral issues are.

All these citizen science projects aim to improve dog health and behavior. Dog owners around the world can give scientists data. This work helps dogs and people enjoy happier, healthier lives.

Further Evidence

Look at the website below. Does it give any new evidence to support Chapter Three?

The Canine Brains Project

abdocorelibrary.com/dog-projects

Science Projects

Dog owners can sign up online to participate in dog research as citizen scientists.

Owners may answer lots of questions about their dogs.

Owners may swab their dogs' mouths to get DNA to send to researchers.

Owners may take their dogs to a vet to get blood samples.

Glossary

aggression
actions that are very unfriendly or harmful to others

behavior
the way a person or animal acts

canine
related to dogs

data
information

DNA
deoxyribonucleic acid, a tiny part of the body that holds information about a living thing

environment
the surroundings in which a person or animal lives

genetics
the traits that are passed down to a living thing, such as appearance, behavior, and health

habits
usual or routine actions

Online Resources

To learn more about dogs and dog projects, visit our free resource websites below.

Visit **abdocorelibrary.com** or scan this QR code for free Common Core resources for teachers and students, including vetted activities, multimedia, and booklinks, for deeper subject comprehension.

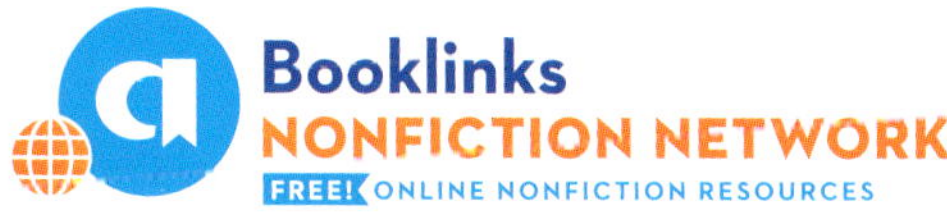

Visit **abdobooklinks.com** or scan this QR code for free additional online weblinks for further learning. These links are routinely monitored and updated to provide the most current information available.

Learn More

Donohue, Moira Rose, and Stephanie Gibeault. *Can't Get Enough Dog Stuff.* National Geographic Kids, 2023.

Miller, Marie-Therese. *Dogs.* Abdo, 2023.

Index

About the Author

Marie Pearson is an author and editor of books for young readers. She has shared her life with seven dogs and is currently living with a standard poodle and a miniature dachshund. She takes dog research surveys to help improve the lives of dogs and their people.